Team Spirit ®

THE NEW YORK RANGERS

BY

MARK STEWART

Content Consultant
Denis Gibbons
Society for International Hockey Research

NORWOOD HOUSE PRESS

CHICAGO, ILLINOIS

Norwood House Press
P.O. Box 316598
Chicago, Illinois 60631

For information regarding Norwood House Press, please visit our website at:
www.norwoodhousepress.com or call 866-565-2900.

PHOTO CREDITS:
All photos courtesy Getty Images except the following:
Topps, Inc. (6, 16, 20, 30, 34 right, 35 top left, 36, 40 bottom left, 41 top & bottom right),
Black Book Partners (7, 9), McDiarmid/Cartophilium (14, 34 left),
Associated Press (19, 27, 35 top right, 39), Doug MacLellan/Hockey Hall of Fame (28),
Imperial Oil - Turofsky/Hockey Hall of Fame (31), Beehive Corn Syrup (29),
Author's Collection (17, 38, 40 bottom, 41 left), Société de Publication Merlin (21),
O-Pee-Chee, Ltd. (22, 43), GOAL Magazine/NHL Services (37),
Toronto Sun (40 top left).
Cover photo: Noah Graham/Getty Images
Special thanks to Topps, Inc.

Editor: Mike Kennedy
Designer: Ron Jaffe
Project Management: Black Book Partners, LLC.
Research: Joshua Zaffos
Special thanks to Jeff and Ryan Beebe

LIBRARY OF CONGRESS CATALOGING-IN-PUBLICATION DATA

Stewart, Mark, 1960-
  The New York Rangers / by Mark Stewart.
    p. cm. -- (Team spirit)
  Includes bibliographical references and index.
  Summary: "Presents the history and accomplishments of the New York
Rangers hockey team. Includes highlights of players, coaches, and awards,
quotes, timeline, maps, glossary and websites"--Provided by publisher.
  ISBN-13: 978-1-59953-339-1 (library edition : alk. paper)
  ISBN-10: 1-59953-339-1 (library edition : alk. paper) 1. New York
Rangers (Hockey team)--History--Juvenile literature. I. Title.
  GV848.N43S74 2010
  796.962'647471--dc22
                                                    2009018003

COVER PHOTO: The Rangers celebrate a victory during the 2008–09 season.

Table of Contents

SPORTS WORDS & VOCABULARY WORDS: In this book, you will find many words that are new to you. You may also see familiar words used in new ways. The glossary on page 46 gives the meanings of hockey words, as well as "everyday" words that have special hockey meanings. These words appear in **bold type** throughout the book. The glossary on page 47 gives the meanings of vocabulary words that are not related to hockey. They appear in ***bold italic type*** throughout the book.

Meet the Rangers

For sports teams in New York City, each game can seem like a matter of life and death. Fans in the "Big Apple" know what it takes to be a winner, and they demand maximum effort from their players at all times. The New York Rangers are no exception. The "Broadway Blueshirts" are expected to play their best every time they take the ice.

Like any **National Hockey League (NHL)** team, the Rangers try to fill their **roster** with fast skaters and good shooters. But the fans want more than that. They love to cheer for players who also make smart passes, hard checks, and dive in front of enemy shots.

This book tells the story of the Rangers. They have had some of the greatest stars in hockey and some of the most loyal fans in all of sports. Through more than 80 years of ups and downs, the Rangers have held a special place in the hearts of New Yorkers and in the history of New York.

Scott Gomez and Chris Drury celebrate a goal during a 2008–09 game.

Way Back When

ALL-TIME GREATS

FRANK BOUCHER

ex Rickard was one of America's most famous sportsmen. In 1925, he built an arena on the West Side of New York City and called it Madison Square Garden. A short time later, he decided the building should have its own hockey team. The New York Rangers joined the NHL for the 1926–27 season.

Rickard hired Conn Smythe and Lester Patrick to assemble his team. New York's early stars included Frank Boucher, and the Cook brothers, Bill and Fred, whose nickname was "Bun." Together they formed the high-scoring "Bread Line." The defense was *anchored* by Ching Johnson. Patrick took over as coach, and the Rangers won the **Stanley Cup** in their second season. They repeated as champions in 1933.

By the end of the 1930s, Patrick's two sons—Lynn and Muzz— were stars for the Rangers. So were two other brothers, Neil and Mac Colville. Along with Phil Watson, Bryan Hextall, and goalie Davey Kerr, they made the Rangers almost unbeatable. New York won the Stanley Cup in 1940, with Boucher coaching the team.

ABOVE: Frank Boucher, who won three Stanley Cups with the Rangers.
RIGHT: Jean Ratelle, the center of New York's famous "GAG" line.

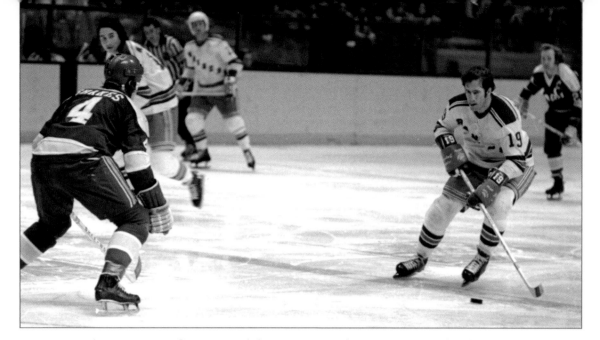

In the years after World War II, the Rangers had some great players, but they tumbled in the **standings**. The team's stars during this *era* included Andy Bathgate and Dean Prentice. Goalie Gump Worsley and Harry Howell led the defense.

In the late 1960s, the Rangers rose to greatness again. Goalie Ed Giacomin and defenseman Brad Park protected the New York net. Jean Ratelle, Rod Gilbert, and Vic Hadfield formed the "GAG" line. They earned this nickname because they were usually good for a "Goal a Game." In 1972, the Rangers reached the **Stanley Cup Finals**.

A new **lineup** led the team back to the finals in 1979. New York's stars were Phil Esposito, Don Maloney, Ron Greschner, Carol Vadnais, Ron Duguay, John Davidson, and two fast-skating Swedes, Ulf Nilsson and Anders Hedberg. Over the next several seasons, Craig Patrick (Lester's grandson) ran the team, and Herb Brooks was the Rangers'

most famous coach. New York blended European and North American styles to create a whole new kind of hockey.

In the 1990s, the Rangers returned to the top of the NHL. Their leader on defense was Brian Leetch. He was joined by a creative **playmaker** named Sergei Zubov. Mike Richter was a fearless young goalie. On the front line, Adam Graves was a hard-hitting forward with a

good scoring touch. The team captain was Mark Messier. When Mike Keenan arrived to coach the Rangers in 1993–94, they ended 54 years of disappointment with a thrilling championship.

Wayne Gretzky joined the team two years later, and it looked as if the Rangers were ready to build a *dynasty*. But age and injuries kept them from reaching their *potential*. The Rangers continued to add big stars, including Pat LaFontaine, Theo Fleury, Eric Lindros, and Pavel Bure. This *strategy* backfired. Instead of ruling the NHL, the Rangers failed to reach the **playoffs** seven years in a row starting in 1997–98. The great **team chemistry** of 1994 was gone. It was time for a new *generation* to take over.

LEFT: Brian Leetch handles the puck in his own end of the ice.
ABOVE: Mark Messier, the star who led the Rangers to the 1994 Stanley Cup.

The Team Today

For many years, the Rangers believed that the best way to win games and entertain their fans was to build the team around famous players. Unfortunately, this plan didn't work. New York couldn't find the right recipe for success. The Rangers struggled year after year.

Finally, the Rangers tried a new *formula*. They **drafted** and traded for talented young players such as Marc Staal, Nikolai Zherdev, Brandon Dubinsky, and Henrik Lundqvist. They signed older players who had experience in the playoffs, including Markus Naslund, Scott Gomez, and Chris Drury.

The fans didn't mind cheering for a team that was "missing" superstars and **Hall of Famers**. In fact, they loved it. The Rangers quickly got back on the winning track. With a new cast of stars and **role players**, the team began to win close, exciting games with maximum effort and great team spirit. The Rangers and their fans set their sights on the Stanley Cup once again.

Nikolai Zherdev and Markus Naslund congratulate each other after a goal during a 2008–09 game.

Home Ice

The Rangers have had two homes during their long history. Both were named Madison Square Garden. But while the team earned the nickname the "Broadway Blueshirts," neither arena was on Broadway, which is Manhattan's most famous street. Nor was either arena anywhere near Madison Square. The arenas were actually named after a well-known New York building that dated back to the 1800s.

From 1926 to 1968, the Rangers played in the Madison Square Garden on 50th Street and 8th Avenue. Starting in the 1940s, they shared the arena with the Knicks basketball team. Their current home is also on 8th Avenue, 17 blocks away from the site of the original arena. The Knicks play there, too.

BY THE NUMBERS

- *There are 18,200 seats for hockey in the Rangers' arena.*
- *The Rangers' arena is the fourth building called Madison Square Garden. The first was built in 1879.*
- *The first sports event held in the current Rangers' arena was a basketball game between the Knicks and the San Diego Rockets. New York won 114–102.*

Former players gather at center ice in Madison Square Garden for a ceremony to retire the number of Adam Graves.

Dressed for Success

The Rangers' sweater has changed little over the 80-plus years since the team first took the ice. New York's colors have always been red, white, and blue. When the Rangers wear their blue sweater, the team name is spelled out diagonally in red letters. When the players wear white, the lettering is blue. The Rangers were the first team to match their gloves to their uniforms. They have worn red, white, and blue gloves since 1957–58.

The team has experimented with different designs and *logos* from time to time. In the late 1970s, the Rangers had a shield on the front of their sweaters. In the 1990s, the sweater showed the head of the Statue of Liberty. The Rangers wear blue at home and white on the road, and their helmet color matches their sweaters. The team wears red pants in every game.

A trading card shows Neil Colville in New York's home uniform from the 1940s.

UNIFORM BASICS

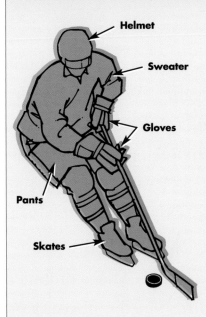

Helmet

Sweater

Gloves

Pants

Skates

The hockey uniform has five important parts:
- Helmet
- Sweater
- Pants
- Gloves
- Skates

Hockey helmets are made of hard plastic with softer padding inside. Some players also wear visors to protect their eyes.

The hockey uniform top is called a sweater. Players wear padding underneath it to protect their shoulders, spine, and ribs. Padded hockey pants, or "breezers," extend from the waist to the knees. Players also wear padding on their knees and shins.

Hockey gloves protect the top of the hand and the wrist. Only a thin layer of leather covers the palm, which helps a player control his stick. A goalie wears two different gloves—one for catching pucks and one for blocking them. Goalies also wear heavy leg pads and a mask. They paint their masks to match their personalities and team colors.

All players wear hockey skates. The blade is curved at each end. The skate "boot" is made from metal, plastic, nylon, and either real or *synthetic* leather. Goalies wear skates that have extra protection on the toe and ankle.

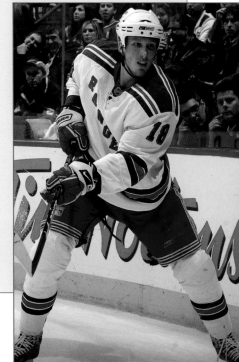

Marc Staal wears the Rangers' 2008–09 road uniform.

We Won!

ALL-TIME GREATS

LESTER PATRICK

When the Rangers joined the NHL, they were able to build quickly with stars from the struggling **Western Hockey League (WHL)**. Frank Boucher, Bill Cook, and Bun Cook came from the WHL. So did New York's coach, Lester Patrick. Goalie Lorne Chabot joined the Rangers after playing for a small-town team in Canada.

In 1927–28, Boucher and the Cooks formed the league's top line. They combined for 55 goals in 44 games. In the **postseason**, the Rangers beat the Pittsburgh Pirates and Boston Bruins to reach the Stanley Cup Finals against the Montreal Maroons.

Because the circus was performing in Madison Square Garden, the finals had to be played in Montreal. The Rangers dropped Game 1. When Chabot suffered an eye injury in Game 2, New York was in deep trouble. Teams did not carry extra goalies in those days. The white-haired Patrick had no choice but to tend goal himself.

Patrick was amazing, stopping all but one shot. Boucher scored in **overtime** for a *dramatic* victory. The Rangers rolled from there.

Joe Miller took over for Patrick, and New York won its first Stanley Cup. Boucher was the star of the playoffs, with seven goals.

By 1933, New York's stars were all aging. But as the playoffs began, Boucher and the Cook brothers got their second wind. They beat the Montreal Canadiens and Detroit Red Wings to set up a championship showdown with the young and powerful Toronto Maple Leafs. The Rangers won the Stanley Cup on an overtime goal by Bill Cook in Game 4. It was the first time in NHL history that the championship was decided in "OT."

New York captured its next title in 1940. The Rangers no longer had a team full of superstars, but they still had plenty of talent. Bryan Hextall was one of the NHL's fastest skaters. Neil Colville was a great scorer. Goalie Davey Kerr played his best when the Rangers had their backs against the wall. After a tough series win over the Boston Bruins, New York faced a championship rematch with Toronto.

The Rangers and Leafs were evenly matched. Hextall scored a **hat trick** in Game 2 to give New York a win and the series lead. But

LEFT: Lester Patrick, the coach and emergency goalie for the 1927–28 champs.   **ABOVE**: A team photo of the 1940 champs.

Toronto tied it up with back-to-back victories. The Rangers won the next two games—and the Stanley Cup— on overtime goals by Muzz Patrick and Hextall.

No one could have imagined it then, but more than 50 years would pass before the Rangers hoisted the Stanley Cup again. In 1993–94, three superstars joined forces to make the Rangers champions. Mark Messier was an *inspirational* leader who could lift his teammates when they were down. Brian Leetch was an excellent defenseman who scored like a forward. Goalie Mike Richter was one of the best in the game.

Under coach Mike Keenan, these stars blended with a strong supporting cast. The Rangers finished the season with the NHL's best record. They played with great confidence in playoff victories over the New York Islanders and Washington Capitals. In the **Eastern Conference Finals**, New York trailed the New Jersey Devils. But the Rangers rallied to win the series on Stephane Matteau's dramatic goal in Game 7.

The Rangers faced the Vancouver Canucks in the Stanley Cup Finals. New York fans worried when their team lost Game 1. But the Rangers responded by taking three games in a row. The Canucks battled back to force Game 7 in New York. Leetch gave the Rangers a 1–0 lead with a goal in the first period, and Richter made several incredible saves in the third period. New York celebrated a 3–2 victory—

and its fourth Stanley Cup! Leetch won the Conn Smythe Trophy as the top performer of the playoffs.

Many elderly Rangers fans had feared they might never live long enough to see their team lift the Cup again. After the final siren sounded, one fan held a sign that read: NOW I CAN DIE IN PEACE.

LEFT: Jeff Beukeboom and Steve Larmer celebrate with Stephane Matteau after his goal to beat the New Jersey Devils.
ABOVE: Mike Richter reaches to make a glove save in Game 7 against the Vancouver Canucks.

Go-To Guys

To be a true star in the NHL, you need more than a great slapshot. You have to be a "go-to guy"—someone teammates trust to make the winning play when the seconds are ticking away in a big game. Rangers fans have had a lot to cheer about over the years, including these great stars …

THE PIONEERS

FRANK BOUCHER   Center

- BORN: OCTOBER 7, 1902 • DIED: DECEMBER 12, 1977
- PLAYED FOR TEAM: 1926–27 TO 1937–38 & 1943–44

Frank Boucher was one of hockey's greatest playmakers. He was also one of the game's true gentlemen. Boucher won the Lady Byng Trophy for sportsmanship so often that the league let him keep the trophy, and then made a new one!

BILL COOK   Right Wing

- BORN: OCTOBER 8, 1895 • DIED: APRIL 6, 1986
- PLAYED FOR TEAM: 1926–27 TO 1936–37

Bill Cook was the first player signed by the Rangers, and he scored their first goal. In 1932–33, Cook led the NHL with 50 points (28 goals plus 22 **assists**) in 48 games. At age 36, he was the league's oldest scoring champ.

ABOVE: Bill Cook   **RIGHT**: Rod Gilbert and Jean Ratelle surround Camille Henry on the cover of a French-Canadian hockey magazine.

ANDY BATHGATE   Right Wing

• BORN: AUGUST 28, 1932 • PLAYED FOR TEAM: 1952–53 TO 1963–64

Andy Bathgate was a great leader. Even though the Rangers missed the playoffs in 1958–59, he still won the Hart Trophy as the league's top performer. Bathgate had one of the NHL's hardest shots. He once set a record by scoring a goal in 10 games in a row.

JEAN RATELLE   Center

• BORN: OCTOBER 3, 1940

• PLAYED FOR TEAM: 1960–61 TO 1975–76

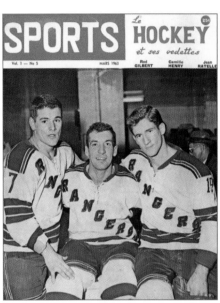

Jean Ratelle was one of the best **all-around** athletes in the NHL. He could have played **professional** baseball or golf. His choice of hockey was smart. Ratelle became one of the most beloved and respected Rangers.

ROD GILBERT   Right Wing

• BORN: JULY 1, 1941

• PLAYED FOR TEAM: 1960–61 TO 1977–78

Hockey is very hard to play with a back injury, but Rod Gilbert fought through the pain. During his career, he needed two major back operations to continue playing. He scored over 400 goals for the Rangers and retired with more than 1,000 points.

ED GIACOMIN   Goalie

• BORN: JUNE 6, 1939 • PLAYED FOR TEAM: 1965–66 TO 1975–76

The Rangers made the playoffs nine times during Ed Giacomin's 10 years as a starter. He led the NHL in wins three times. Giacomin was so quick that fans nicknamed him "Fast Eddie."

BRAD PARK   Defenseman

- BORN: JULY 6, 1948   • PLAYED FOR TEAM: 1968–69 TO 1975–76

Brad Park was one of the NHL's best "offensive" defensemen. He was also superb in his own end of the rink. Instead of slamming into forwards, Park muscled them to spots on the ice where they could not get off good shots.

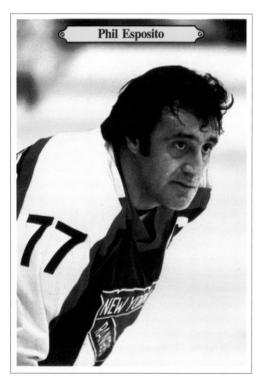

Phil Esposito

PHIL ESPOSITO   Center

- BORN: FEBRUARY 20, 1942
- PLAYED FOR TEAM: 1975–76 TO 1980–81

Phil Esposito was a record-breaking scorer with the Boston Bruins before the Rangers traded Jean Ratelle and Brad Park to get him. "Espo" was also a *dynamic* leader. He guided the Rangers to the Stanley Cup Finals in 1979.

BRIAN LEETCH   Defenseman

- BORN: MARCH 3, 1968
- PLAYED FOR TEAM: 1987–88 TO 2003–04

Brian Leetch was a top defenseman and an equally talented offensive player. He had a hard, accurate shot and was a skilled passer. Leetch won the Norris Trophy twice as the NHL's top defenseman and set a record for first-year defensemen with 23 goals.

ABOVE: Phil Esposito   **RIGHT**: Henrik Lundqvist

MIKE RICHTER
Goalie

- BORN: SEPTEMBER 22, 1966 • PLAYED FOR TEAM: 1989–90 TO 2002–03

The more pressure opponents put on Mike Richter, the calmer he seemed to get. His great play in 1993–94 was a key to the Rangers' long-awaited Stanley Cup. Richter and Brian Leetch were two of the top American stars in the NHL during the 1990s.

MARK MESSIER
Center

- BORN: JANUARY 18, 1961
- PLAYED FOR TEAM: 1991–92 TO 1996–97 & 2000–01 TO 2003–04

When hockey experts are asked to name the game's greatest leaders, Mark Messier is always at the top of the list. He was a fierce and focused player who lifted the Rangers to the top of the NHL. Messier scored 107 points in his first season in New York.

HENRIK LUNDQVIST
Goalie

- BORN: MARCH 2, 1982
- FIRST SEASON WITH TEAM: 2005–06

Henrik Lundqvist continued New York's *tradition* of great goaltenders. He won at least 30 games in each of his first three seasons and recorded 10 **shutouts** in 2007–08. The following season, he played in the **All-Star Game** for the first time.

Behind the Bench

The Rangers have had more than 30 coaches in their history. Among the best were Lester Patrick, Emile Francis, Fred Shero, Herb Brooks, Mike Keenan, and Roger Neilson. All rank among the finest coaches in NHL history. Many former star players have also coached the team, including Frank Boucher, Bill Cook, Neil Colville, Phil Watson, Phil Esposito, and Glen Sather.

Patrick led the Rangers to the Stanley Cup in 1928 and 1933. He was very good at *motivating* his players. He also encouraged his three top scorers—Boucher, Bill Cook, and Bun Cook—to practice their passing and shooting separately from the team. This helped them experiment with plays that made them the best line in the NHL.

Keenan only coached the Rangers for a year—but what a year it was! He whipped his players into championship form and made them believe they were unbeatable. The Rangers won 52 games in 1993–94 and won the Stanley Cup in a thrilling seven-game series. Keenan was nicknamed "Iron Mike" because he was so demanding.

Mike Keenan and his players are the picture of joy after their 1994 Stanley Cup Championship.

One Great Day

The **rivalry** between the Rangers and New Jersey Devils is one of hockey's most heated. Things got especially hot during the 1994 Eastern Conference Finals. The Rangers were expected to win the Stanley Cup that year, but they trailed the Devils after five games.

New York captain Mark Messier knew he had to do something to get the attention of his teammates. The night before Game 6 in New Jersey, he told reporters, "We know we have to win it. We can win it. And we are *going* to win it."

The problem was that the Devils and their fans read the newspapers, too. By game time, every New Jersey player vowed they would teach Messier and the Rangers a lesson: You never *ever* guarantee a victory in sports. With Devils fans screaming at the top of their lungs, New Jersey built a 2–0 lead in the third period. Messier realized that he would have to take his game to a new level.

The Rangers made the score 2–1 when Messier flicked a pass to Alexei Kovalev, who shot the puck past goalie Martin Brodeur. The Rangers tied the score when Messier took a hard pass from Kovalev and tucked the puck under Brodeur's legs. New York took a 3–2 lead when

Mark Messier watches the puck zip past Martin Brodeur for his game-winning goal.

Messier won a faceoff and then headed for the net. Brodeur stopped a shot by Kovalev, but Messier banged in the rebound.

With time running out, the Devils pulled the goalie. Messier stopped a pass in front of his goal, looked up, and saw New Jersey's wide-open net. He calmly sent the puck skidding down the ice for his third goal of the game.

No one was happier than Messier about the Rangers' win. Two nights later, New York beat New Jersey in Game 7 in Madison Square Garden. The Rangers went on to win the Stanley Cup. The championship may have been "expected," but no one imagined the road to victory would be so bumpy.

Legend Has It

Which Ranger got the best "trade-in" on his car?

LEGEND HAS IT that Mike Richter did. Richter was not a flashy guy. He lived *modestly*, dressed simply, and saw no reason to drive anything other than his beat-up old Honda—until the 1994 All-Star Game. Richter made several great saves in the contest and was named MVP. His prize was a new pickup truck. Two years later, Richter got another new set of wheels. This time he was named MVP of the hockey **World Cup** and won a motorcycle.

ABOVE: Mike Richter shows off a new set of "hot wheels."
RIGHT: Andy Bathgate, the inventor of the curved hockey stick.

Which Ranger invented the curved hockey stick?

Andy Bathgate

LEGEND HAS IT that Andy Bathgate did. Bathgate actually began experimenting with this *technique* before he became a pro. He soaked the blade of his stick in hot water, bent it, and then let it dry overnight. Bathgate found that shooting with a curved stick made the puck do strange things in the air. Soon other NHL players were using curved sticks. Eventually, the league had to limit the curve of a stick for the safety of the goalies.

Which Ranger was a baseball hero before he played pro hockey?

LEGEND HAS IT that Chris Drury was. In 2008, Drury was named New York's captain. He was just the second American-born captain in team history. Nearly two *decades* earlier, Drury was a star in a different sport. In 1989, he led the baseball team from his hometown of Trumbull, Connecticut to the Little League World Series. Trumbull won the championship thanks to Drury's pitching and hitting.

It Really Happened

The secret dream of every NHL goalie is to score a goal. In Chuck Rayner's case, it was no secret at all. He was always on the lookout for an opportunity to put the puck in the net. In all of his years with the Rangers, Rayner never had a winning record.

Still, he was the most athletic and agile goalie in the league. In 1949–50, he went 28–30–11 and helped the Rangers reach the Stanley Cup Finals.

Rayner loved to join the Rangers' attack. He would skate to the other end of the ice when the referees called a **delayed penalty** on an opponent, hoping to surprise the goalie with a shot. Rayner's tactics shocked people in arenas around the league, but the fans in Madison Square Garden loved watching their goalie transform into an offensive player.

Rayner's best chances to score came when the Rangers were ahead late in the third period. In these situations, the opponent pulled its

ABOVE: A trading card of Chuck Rayner.
RIGHT: Rayner skates from his net to chase down the puck.

goalie off the ice and replaced him with an extra attacker. Many times, Rayner stopped a shot and then quickly slapped the puck toward the open goal at the other end. He came close a few times but never made the shot.

Rayner once played in an exhibition match against the Maritime All-Stars in Canada. Since the game didn't count, he decided this was his big chance to realize his dream. He barreled down the ice with the puck, shouldering opponents out of the way. Once he crossed the opposite blue line, Rayner cut to the net and backhanded a shot past the stunned goalie. He finally had his goal.

More than two decades later, Rayner celebrated another thrilling moment in his career. In 1973, he became just the second goalie in hockey history with a losing record to be voted into the Hall of Fame.

Team Spirit

Every NHL team has its ups and downs, especially one as old as the Rangers. During the good times, every seat in Madison Square Garden is sold, and the fans shout out special chants and cheers all game long. The atmosphere is nearly the same during the bad times. Indeed, it is still hard to get a ticket to a Rangers game, and the arena is just as noisy.

Rangers fans love hockey, and they understand the game. They applaud for players who work hard and do the little things to help the team win. If a player gives less than his all, he can expect to hear from the coaches in the stands—all 18,200 of them. Barry Beck, who starred for the Rangers in the 1980s, said he hated to leave Madison Square Garden after a loss. "My doorman won't even talk to me!" he once claimed.

Among the Rangers' many traditions are special songs that are played after every goal and every win. The team's victory song dates back to 1940. A more recent tradition is a fan called "Dancing Larry." He performs during the third period to get the crowd pumped up. After every victory, the Rangers skate to center ice and raise their sticks to salute the fans.

The Rangers show their appreciation to the New York fans after a win in 2008–09.

Timeline

The hockey season is played from October through June. That means each season takes place at the end of one year and the beginning of the next. In this timeline, the accomplishments of the Rangers are shown by season.

1927–28
The Rangers win the Stanley Cup in their second season.

1976–77
Don Murdoch scores five goals in a game.

1939–40
The Rangers win their third Stanley Cup.

1958–59
Andy Bathgate becomes the team's first 40-goal scorer.

1971–72
The "GAG" line scores 312 points.

Bryan Hextall, a star for the 1940 champs.

Vic Hadfield, a member of the "GAG" line.

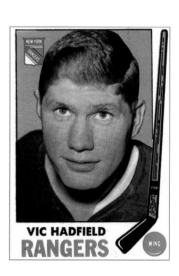

VIC HADFIELD
RANGERS

John
Vanbiesbrouck

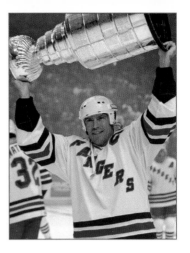

Mark
Messier

1985–86
John Vanbiesbrouck
wins the Vezina Trophy
as the NHL's top goalie.

1993–94
The Rangers win
their first Stanley
Cup in 54 years.

2005–06
Jaromir Jagr sets a team
record with 54 goals.

1991–92
Mark Messier leads
the Rangers to their
first 50-win season.

2001–02
Theo Fleury
scores his 1,000th
career point.

2007–08
Brandon Dubinsky is
named MVP of the
YoungStars Game.

Brandon
Dubinsky

Fun Facts

LAW AND ORDER

Tex Rickard originally wanted to name his team the Giants. But newspaper writers came up with the nickname "Tex's Rangers," which referred to the famous lawmen known as the Texas Rangers. The name stuck, and Rickard went with it.

ED GIACOMIN — GOALIE

OK, WHO'S NEXT?

In 1966–67, Ed Giacomin led the NHL with nine shutouts. He had at least one against every team in the league.

WE'RE RETIRED

In 2009, the Rangers retired the numbers of Adam Graves (#9), Andy Bathgate (#9), and Harry Howell (#3). Their sweaters were hung alongside those of Rod Gilbert (#7), Mike Richter (#35), Brian Leetch (#2), Mark Messier (#11), and Ed Giacomin (#1). Wayne Gretzky's #99 has also been retired by every NHL team.

ABOVE: Ed Giacomin   **RIGHT**: Anders Hedberg and Ulf Nilsson share the cover of a magazine.

SWEDISH CONNECTION

In 1978, the Rangers signed two stars from the **World Hockey Association (WHA)**, Anders Hedberg and Ulf Nilsson. Only two Swedes had played in the NHL before them.

ANDERS HEDBERG / ULF NILSSON
NEW YORK RANGERS

FAMILY MATTERS

Where would the Rangers be without the Patrick family? Lester Patrick coached the team to two Stanley Cups. His sons, Lynn and Muzz, starred for the 1940 Stanley Cup championship team. In the late 1980s, Lynn's son Craig signed many of the players that helped the Rangers win the Stanley Cup in 1994.

TV TIME

The first televised hockey game was in 1940. The Rangers hosted the Montreal Canadiens. The broadcast was an experiment. There were only 300 television sets in New York City at the time.

DON'T GET SO DEFENSIVE

In 1993–94, New York's leading scorer was Sergei Zubov, with 89 points. It was the first time in NHL history a defenseman was the top scorer on a first-place team.

Talking Hockey

"Brian Leetch is such a good hockey player, I am tempted to leave him in all the time."
—*Roger Neilson, on his star defenseman*

"Would it have been fair *not* to give the fans the chance to see my beautiful face?"
—*Gump Worsley, joking about why he never wore a mask*

"Messier only has three speeds—fast, faster, and fastest."
—*Emile Francis, on Mark Messier*

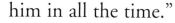

"When you get a little older you realize the playoffs are the real season."

—*Scott Gomez, on the importance of the playoffs*

"A good hockey player plays where the puck is. A great hockey player plays where the puck is going to be."

—*Wayne Gretzky, on what made him one of hockey's greatest players ever*

"They made the game enjoyable for me because we fit together so well."

—*Jean Ratelle, on linemates Rod Gilbert and Vic Hadfield*

"Being a Ranger and playing in Madison Square Garden was more than privilege enough. Tonight's honor is simply overwhelming."

—*Adam Graves, on having his number retired by the Rangers*

"I have been fortunate to win at various levels … But that was the greatest."

—*Mike Keenan, on coaching the Rangers to the Stanley Cup in 1993–94*

LEFT: An autographed photo of Gump Worsley.
ABOVE: Wayne Gretzky

For the Record

T he great Rangers teams and players have left their marks on the record books. These are the "best of the best" …

Gilles Villemure

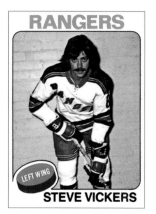

Steve Vickers

RANGERS AWARD WINNERS

HART MEMORIAL TROPHY
MOST VALUABLE PLAYER (MVP)

Buddy O'Connor	1947–48
Chuck Rayner	1949–50
Andy Bathgate	1958–59
Mark Messier	1991–92

VEZINA TROPHY
TOP GOALTENDER

Davey Kerr	1939–40
Ed Giacomin & Gilles Villemure	1970–71
John Vanbiesbrouck	1985–86

JAMES NORRIS MEMORIAL TROPHY
TOP DEFENSIVE PLAYER

Doug Harvey	1961–62
Harry Howell	1966–67
Brian Leetch	1991–92
Brian Leetch	1996–97

ALL-STAR GAME MVP

Don Maloney	1983–84
Mike Gartner	1992–93
Mike Richter	1993–94
Wayne Gretzky	1998–99

CALDER TROPHY
TOP FIRST-YEAR PLAYER

Kilby MacDonald	1939–40
Grant Warwick	1941–42
Edgar Laprade	1945–46
Pentti Lund	1948–49
Gump Worsley	1952–53
Camille Henry	1953–54
Steve Vickers	1972–73
Brian Leetch	1988–89

CONN SMYTHE TROPHY
MVP DURING PLAYOFFS

Brian Leetch	1993–94

A pennant from the 1993–94 season, when the Rangers hosted the All-Star Game.

RANGERS ACHIEVEMENTS

ACHIEVEMENT	SEASON
Stanley Cup Champions	1927–28
Stanley Cup Finalists	1928–29
Stanley Cup Finalists	1931–32
Stanley Cup Champions	1932–33
Stanley Cup Finalists	1936–37
Stanley Cup Champions	1939–40
Stanley Cup Finalists	1949–50
Stanley Cup Finalists	1971–72
Stanley Cup Finalists	1978–79
Stanley Cup Champions	1993–94

Harry Howell Defense
NEW YORK RANGERS

BRAD PARK DEFENSE

LEFT: Davey Kerr, the goalie for the 1940 champs.
TOP: Harry Howell, the NHL's top defender in 1966–67.
ABOVE: Brad Park, a star for the 1971–72 team.

Pinpoints

T he history of a hockey team is made up of many smaller stories. These stories take place all over the map—not just in the city a team calls "home." Match the pushpins on these maps to the Team Facts and you will begin to see the story of the Rangers unfold!

TEAM FACTS

1 New York, New York—*The Rangers have played here since 1926–27.*

2 Abington, Pennsylvania—*Mike Richter was born here.*

3 Corpus Christi, Texas—*Brian Leetch was born here.*

4 Kansas City, Missouri—*Tex Rickard was born here.*

5 Detroit, Michigan—*John Vanbiesbrouck was born here.*

6 Anchorage, Alaska—*Scott Gomez was born here.*

7 Montreal, Quebec, Canada—*Rod Gilbert was born here.*

8 Toronto, Ontario, Canada—*Adam Graves was born here.*

9 Winnipeg, Manitoba, Canada—*Andy Bathgate was born here.*

10 Sutherland, Saskatchewan, Canada—*Chuck Rayner was born here.*

11 Moscow, Russia—*Sergei Zubov was born here.*

12 Kladno, Czech Republic—*Jaromir Jagr was born here.*

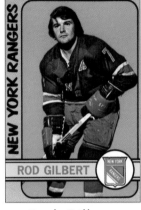

Rod Gilbert

Faceoff

Hockey is played between two teams of five skaters and a goalie. Each team has two defensemen and a forward line that includes a left wing, right wing, and center. The goalie's job is to stop the puck from crossing the red goal line. A hockey goal is 6 feet (1.8 meters) wide and 4 feet (1.2 meters) high. The hockey puck is a round disk made of hard rubber. It weighs approximately 6 ounces.

During a game, players work hard for a full "shift." When they get tired, they take a seat on the bench, and a new group jumps off the bench and over the boards to take their place (except for the goalie). Forwards play together in set groups, or "lines," and defensemen do, too.

There are rules that prevent players from injuring or interfering with opponents. However, players are allowed to bump, or "check," each other when they battle for the puck. Because hockey is a fast game played by strong athletes, sometimes checks can be rough!

If a player breaks a rule, a penalty is called by one of two referees. For most penalties, the player must sit in the penalty box for two minutes. This gives the other team a one-skater advantage, or "power play." The team down a skater is said to be "short-handed."

NHL games have three 20-minute periods—60 minutes in all—and the team that scores the most goals is the winner. If the score is tied, the teams play an overtime period. The first team to score during overtime wins. If the game is still tied, it is decided by a shootout—a one-on-one contest between the goalies and the best shooters from the other team. During the Stanley Cup playoffs, no shootouts are held. The teams play until the tie is broken.

Things happen so quickly in hockey that it is easy to overlook set plays. The next time you watch a game, see if you can spot these plays:

PLAY LIST

DEFLECTION—Sometimes a shooter does not try to score a goal. Instead, he aims his shot so that a teammate can touch the puck with his stick and suddenly change its direction. If the goalie is moving to stop the first shot, he may be unable to adjust to the "deflection."

GIVE-AND-GO—When a skater is closely guarded and cannot get an open shot, he sometimes passes to a teammate with the idea of getting a return pass in better position to shoot. The "give-and-go" works when the defender turns to follow the pass and loses track of his man. By the time he recovers, it is too late.

ONE-TIMER—When a player receives a pass, he often has to control the puck and position himself for a shot. This gives the defense a chance to react. Some players are skilled enough to shoot the instant a pass arrives for a "one-timer." A well-aimed one-timer is almost impossible to stop.

PULLING THE GOALIE—Sometimes in the final moments of a game, the team that is behind will try a risky play. To gain an extra skater, the team will pull the goalie out of the game and replace him with a center, wing, or defenseman. This gives the team a better chance to score. It also leaves the goal unprotected and allows the opponent a chance to score an "empty-net goal."

Glossary

HOCKEY WORDS TO KNOW

ALL-AROUND—Good at all parts of the game.

ALL-STAR GAME—The annual game featuring the NHL's best players. Prior to 1967, the game was played at the beginning of the season between the league champion and an All-Star squad.

ASSISTS—Passes that lead to a goal.

DELAYED PENALTY—A penalty that does not take effect until the penalized team gains control of the puck.

DRAFTED—Chosen from a group of the best junior hockey, college, and international players. The NHL draft is held each summer.

EASTERN CONFERENCE FINALS—The series that determines which team from the East will face the best team from the West in the Stanley Cup Finals.

HALL OF FAMERS—Players who have been honored as being among the greatest ever and are enshrined in the Hockey Hall of Fame.

HAT TRICK—Three goals in one game.

LINEUP—The list of players who are playing in a game.

NATIONAL HOCKEY LEAGUE (NHL)—The league that began play in 1917–18 and is still in existence today.

OVERTIME—The extra period played when a game is tied after 60 minutes.

PLAYMAKER—A player who creates scoring opportunities.

PLAYOFFS—The games played after the season to determine the league champion.

POSTSEASON—Another term for playoffs.

PROFESSIONAL—A player or team that plays a sport for money.

ROLE PLAYERS—Players who have a specific job when they are on the ice.

ROSTER—The list of a team's active players.

SHUTOUTS—Games in which a team is prevented from scoring.

STANDINGS—A daily list of teams, starting with the team with the best record and ending with the team with the worst record.

STANLEY CUP—The championship trophy of North American hockey since 1893, and of the NHL since 1927.

STANLEY CUP FINALS—The series that determines the NHL champion each season. It has been a best-of-seven series since 1939.

TEAM CHEMISTRY—The way players work together on and off the ice. Winning teams usually have good chemistry.

WESTERN HOCKEY LEAGUE (WHL)—A rival league to the NHL in the 1920s. The WHL was called the Western Canada Hockey League until 1925, when a team from Portland, Oregon joined. The WHL went out of business in 1926.

WORLD CUP—A competition between the world's best national teams. The World Cup replaced the Canada Cup, which began in 1976.

WORLD HOCKEY ASSOCIATION (WHA)—A rival league to the NHL that played from 1972–73 through 1978–79. When the WHA went out of business, four of its teams joined the NHL.

YOUNGSTARS GAME—A game between the NHL's best young players, held the day before the All-Star Game.

OTHER WORDS TO KNOW

ANCHORED—Held steady.

DECADES—Periods of 10 years; also specific periods, such as the 1950s.

DRAMATIC—Sudden or surprising.

DYNAMIC—Exciting and energetic.

DYNASTY—A family, group, or team that maintains power over time.

ERA—A period of time in history.

FORMULA—A set way of doing something.

GENERATION—A group of people born during the same period of history.

INSPIRATIONAL—Giving positive and confident feelings to others.

LOGOS—Symbols or designs that represent a company or team.

MODESTLY—Without attracting attention.

MOTIVATING—Inspiring to achieve.

POTENTIAL—The ability to become better.

RIVALRY—Extremely emotional competition.

STRATEGY—A plan or method for succeeding.

SYNTHETIC—Made in a laboratory, not in nature.

TECHNIQUE—A specific way of doing something.

TRADITION—A belief or custom that is handed down from generation to generation.

Places to Go

ON THE ROAD

NEW YORK RANGERS
2 Pennsylvania Plaza
New York, New York 10121
(212) 465-6000

THE HOCKEY HALL OF FAME
Brookfield Place
30 Yonge Street
Toronto, Ontario, Canada   M5E 1X8
(416) 360-7765

ON THE WEB

THE NATIONAL HOCKEY LEAGUE   www.nhl.com
  • *Learn more about the National Hockey League*

THE NEW YORK RANGERS   rangers.nhl.com
  • *Learn more about the Rangers*

THE HOCKEY HALL OF FAME   www.hhof.com
  • *Learn more about hockey's greatest players*

ON THE BOOKSHELF

To learn more about the sport of hockey, look for these books at your library or bookstore:

  • MacDonald, James. *Hockey Skills: How to Play Like a Pro*. Berkeley Heights, New Jersey: Enslow Elementary, 2009.

  • Keltie, Thomas. *Inside Hockey! The legends, facts, and feats that made the game*. Toronto, Ontario, Canada: Maple Tree Press, 2008.

  • Romanuk, Paul. *Scholastic Canada Book of Hockey Lists*. Markham, Ontario, Canada: Scholastic Canada, 2007.

Index

PAGE NUMBERS IN **BOLD** REFER TO ILLUSTRATIONS.

The Team

MARK STEWART has written over 200 books for kids—and more than a dozen books on hockey, including a history of the Stanley Cup and an authorized biography of goalie Martin Brodeur. He grew up in New York City during the 1960s rooting for the Rangers and now lives in New Jersey, where he attends Devils games at the new Prudential Center. He especially likes the special all-you-can-eat seating section. Mark comes from a family of writers. His grandfather was Sunday Editor of *The New York Times* and his mother was Articles Editor of *The Ladies' Home Journal* and *McCall's*. Mark has profiled hundreds of athletes over the last 20 years. He has also written several books about New York and New Jersey. Mark is a graduate of Duke University, with a degree in History. He lives with his daughters and wife Sarah overlooking Sandy Hook, New Jersey.

DENIS GIBBONS is a writer and editor with *The Hockey News* and a former newsletter editor of the Toronto-based Society for International Hockey Research (SIHR). He was a contributing writer to the publication *Kings of the Ice: A History of World Hockey* and has worked as chief hockey researcher at five Winter Olympics for the ABC, CBS, and NBC television networks. Denis also has worked as a researcher for the FOX Sports Network during the Stanley Cup playoffs. He resides in Burlington, Ontario, Canada with his wife Chris.